Hummingbirds

A Celebration of Nature's
Most Dazzling Creatures

BEN SONDER

COURAGE BOOKS

AN IMPRINT OF RUNNING PRESS
PHILADELPHIA • LONDON

9   8   7   6   5   4   3   2   1
Digit on the right indicates the number of this printing.

Library of Congress Cataloging-in-Publication
Number 98-72525

ISBN 0-7624-0420-5

This book was designed and produced by
TODTRI Book Publishers
P. O. Box 572, New York, NY 10116-0572
Fax: (212) 695-6984
e-mail: todtri@mindspring.com

Author: Ben Sonder

Publisher: Robert M. Tod
Senior Editor: Edward Douglas
Designer: Mark Weinberg
Typesetting: Command-O, NYC

Printed and bound in Singapore

Published by Courage Books, an imprint of
Running Press Book Publishers
125 South Twenty-second Street
Philadelphia, PA 19103-4399

Visit us on the web!
www.runningpress.com

PICTURE CREDITS

Dembinsky Photo Associates
Battles 27
Anthony Mercieca 21, 24–25, 62 (top)
Stan Osolinski 67

Jeff Foott Productions
Windland Rice 11, 51

Photo Researchers, Inc. 6
Nick Bergkessel 16, 45, 75
Bonnie Sue 47
Paulo Bonino 44 (bottom), 52, 53
Stephen Dalton 8–9, 26 (top), 46
Treat Davidson 17 (top)
Gregory G. Dimijian 32 (top), 44 (top), 49, 54 (top)
Tim Davis 23
Jerry L. Ferrara 38 (bottom), 57, 65 (top)
Kenneth W. Fink 13
S. C. Fried 15
Francois Gohier 20, 59, 68 (bottom)
G. C. Kelley 18, 28, 54 (bottom), 58, 60, 62 (bottom), 63, 64, 68 (top), 79
Stephen J. Krasemann 48, 76 (top)
Robert Lee 31, 36
Bud Lehnhausen 40–41
George D Lepp 34–35
Michael Lustbade 37
Craig K. Lorenz 12
Maslowski 5, 75
Anthony Mercieca 4, 22, 26 (bottom), 29, 39 (top), 55, 56, 61, 69, 71, 72–73, 77, 78
Gary Retherford 19, 39 (bottom)
A. H. Rider 66
Jany Sauvanet 17 (bottom), 30, 42
Jerry Schad 33
Gregory K. Scott 10
R. Van Nostrand 38 (top)
Karl Weidmann 14
Kent Wood 43
Jim Zipp 76 (bottom)

Picture Perfect
Steve Bentsen 65 (bottom)
Joe McDonald 50
Robert Pollock 32 (bottom)
Paul Sterry 7

Tom Stack & Associates
John Cancalosi 70

CONTENTS

INTRODUCTION

HUMMINGBIRDS THROUGHOUT HISTORY

Though tiny and elusive, hummingbirds' unique skills and habits—as well as their often brilliant colorings—have made them a preoccupation of several ancient and contemporary civilizations. These fanciful birds figure prominently in the myths and legends of quite a few American Indian cultures, as well as in the mythology of many Central and South American societies. In the late nineteenth century, hummingbirds achieved prominence among Europeans as well. The often breathtaking, iridescent hues of their feathers were valued as fashion accessories.

Any casual observer with the proper garden plants or with a backyard hummingbird feeder is bound to respond enthusiastically to a visit from one of these tiny creatures. Hummingbirds' ability to hover seemingly motionless in the air, the hypnotic humming sound of their wings, and their penchant for sudden nose dives or instantaneous shifts in flight direction never fail to mesmerize observers. Their knack for disappearing in the blink of an eye makes their fleeting appearances seem like hallucinations, and gives these birds a special, magical quality few other flying creatures possess. As if that weren't enough, hummingbirds' agility can make them seem bold. One may find a hummingbird suddenly perched on a twig just a few inches from one's face, or even poking its beak into an article of one's red-colored clothing, having

ABOVE: A ruby-throated hummingbird feeds on columbine, an attractive perennial found in many parts of the United States. It is available in abundance in the wild, as are such hummingbird-friendly perennials as Indian paintbrush, bleeding heart, and coral bell.

OPPOSITE: The vast majority of hummingbird species is seen in the tropics, particularly around the equator, with an abundance of species found in southern South America, all the way to the tip of the continent. This Jamaican streamertail is named for the lush island it inhabits.

mistaken it for a nectar-laden blossom. Their apparent speed further adds to their charm, even though these birds are far from the fastest on the planet. Their small size and daring aerial exploits, as well as the breathtaking speed of their wing beatings, has given them a reputation as fast flyers, seemingly far beyond their ability.

It is no wonder, then, that these tiny, brilliantly colored birds are so often the subjects of legends, myths, and superstitions that sometimes have little to do with their actual habits or abilities. In parts of modern Central and South America, for example, the hummingbird is still thought to have magical properties. The bodies of dead hummingbirds are desiccated and ground into powders, which are used as amulets to attract love, money, or power.

Such notions of the magical powers of the hummingbird go back centuries. In several Native American cultures, their speedy flight figures in important religious myths. They are associated with the wind, the rain, and other unstoppable natural forces of mysterious origin.

One Mayan legend holds that the hummingbird is actually the sun in disguise, appearing in birdlike form to woo the moon, which is itself disguised as a beautiful maiden. Another Mayan legend claims that the tiny hummingbird was made from the feathers and body parts left over from the construction of other birds. When the creator beheld the first hummingbirds, a special wedding ceremony was held for them, with the help of spiders and butterflies.

Before the destruction of Aztec civilization by the Spanish, the most powerful Aztec god was associated with the hummingbird. His helmet, fastened to the back of his head, was the head of a hummingbird. Sometimes he wore the helmet covering his head, making him appear as if he were part bird, part man. The god, who was called Huitzilopochtli, was born to a goddess from a ball of hummingbird feathers that had tumbled from the sky.

Early European explorers of the West Indies marveled at the hummingbird, which some mistook for an insect. The fact that the hummingbird only appeared iridescent and jewel-like when its feathers were at certain angles to the sun perplexed and fascinated them. Descriptions of first encounters with them sometimes included a note of trepidation. Tiny as these birds were, they seemed to be very aggressive winged creatures, who flew straight toward the face of an intruder when a nest was disturbed. Columbus wrote about hummingbirds in his diary. A few years later, a hummingbird skin was sent to Rome as a gift for the Pope. Today the Treasure of Milan's Cathedral contains an Episcopal miter decorated with hummer skins, manufactured in Mexico in the third quarter of the sixteenth century.

Because hummingbirds had been unknown on the European continent until the exploration of the West Indies and the Americas, they became, in part, associated with the mystifying wonders and treasures of the New World. Explorers and traders brought them back in captivity for the delight and curiosity of the court. Many ended up desiccated and displayed in glass boxes.

BELOW: The brilliant coloring of birds such as this green violet-eared hummingbird inspired many trends in fashion design. Unfortunately for the birds, this meant the loss of their feathers and their lives to make the gorgeous creations worn by stylish ladies. Many species were brought close to extinction by over-hunting.

LEFT: This rufous-tailed hummingbird, perched on a slender tree branch in Ecuador, is a reminder of the thousands of birds and varied species of all kinds that filled these forests hundreds of years ago. It is easy to understand how some of them played such key roles in Mesoamerican myths.

Finally, in 1758, Linnaeus described eighteen species of hummingbirds in his book *Systema Naturae*. By the middle of the nineteenth century, several monographs on the birds were published by ornithologists and artists.

In the late nineteenth century, Charles Darwin studied hummingbirds, coming to the conclusion that, as in the case of the butterfly, their wings were astoundingly powerful in relation to the size of the rest of their bodies. He tried to analyze their ability to hover, deciding that a fan-like expansion and closing of their tail feathers helped to keep their body in a vertical position.

The late nineteenth century marked a climax in hummingbird exploitation. Not only was the destruction of habitats seriously decreasing the numbers of some species, but a new fashion trend called for the use of hummingbird feathers and bodies on hats, and led to the murder of millions of birds. Those with the most iridescent plumage were favored, and their wing and breast feathers were stripped and pasted together to make new patterns. Sometimes an entire preserved hummingbird topped the feathers and artificial flowers of a lady's hat, positioned to look as if it were hovering, dipping its long beak into a blossom.

It wasn't until the first decade of the twentieth century that the hummingbird craze died down, discouraged by the conservationist efforts of local Audubon groups and other bird lovers.

To this day, legends and superstitions continue to surround these tiny birds. Two of the most common—that hummingbirds die each autumn, only to resurrected in the spring, and that hummingbirds migrate across great bodies of water by hitching rides on the backs of geese—are still so widely believed that most books on hummingbirds feel compelled to debunk them. Despite the increasing body of scientific data that has accumulated about these little creatures, their magical appearance, eccentric habits, and unique abilities continue to stimulate our fantasies.

FOLLOWING PAGE: Though purists believe, and with good reason, that wild creatures are best photographed and documented in their natural habitats, occasional studio shots can be useful. This photograph of a hummingbird approaching some bird-of-paradise blooms dramatically illustrates the diminutive size of the bird.

CHAPTER ONE

EVOLUTION OF THE HUMMINGBIRD

Territory and Environment

The 341 species in the hummingbird family, *Trochilidae*, are all confined to the Western Hemisphere. Their territory reaches all the way from southern Alaska to the tip of South America, but most live along the equator in the rain forests of Columbia and Ecuador, where the flower nectar and insects that they consume are plentiful. Only fifteen species of hummingbird actually breed within the boundaries of the United States. One or another of these species have been seen in forty-nine American states (all except Hawaii) and in ten Canadian provinces. Only the ruby-throated hummingbird *(Archilochus colubris)* makes a home east of the Mississippi, and here it is just a seasonal visitor. This metallic-green bird with a ruby-colored throat is noted for its lengthy migration. Each year it flies nonstop to warmer climates, often across the Gulf of Mexico, a journey that is at least 500 miles (805km).

Migrants

All the other species of North American hummingbirds live in western North America, and many also migrate to Central and South America during the winter. Each year, a few hummingbirds become "laggards" or "strays." Laggards are members of a species that have forgotten to migrate south with other birds. Strays are birds that have fallen out of a migration path and have been found nesting far from their usual region.

ABOVE: This rufous hummingbird, resting quietly near Jackson, Wyoming, may soon be enjoying another spot in southern Texas, after an arduous migration of many hundreds of miles.

OPPOSITE: A ruby-throated hummingbird has perched itself within the branches of an eastern hophornbeam. Though this is the only species that occurs regularly in the eastern United States, it ranges over a vast area.

ABOVE: *Of all the hum-
mingbird species found in
North America, the Anna's
hummingbird is not an ex-
tensive traveler. It may move
from a low lying area to
a nearby higher altitude in
search of more abundant
food, but it does not migrate
outside of its home range.*

OPPOSITE: *The spectacular
red-tailed comet is a denizen
of the temperate northern
Andes. It is not uncommon
to find hummingbirds at
altitudes of over 15,000
feet (4,600m) above sea
level. To escape the lower
nighttime temperatures,
some birds may retreat to
caves, where they enter a
state of torpor until morning.*

Permanent Residents

A few hummingbirds, such as the Anna's hummingbird *(Calypte anna)* of the Pacific Coast and southern Arizona and the Costa's hummingbird *(Calypte costae)* of southern California and Arizona, stay year round in their North American habitats. Also, an increasing number of hummers seem to be following a new practice of wintering in the southeastern United States, near the Gulf of Mexico, in Texas, Florida, Louisiana, Mississippi, and Alabama. As many as fifteen species have been recorded in the Gulf Coast region during winter, although the majority are of the rufous species *(Selsaphorus rufus)* .

Hummingbirds live at diverse altitudes, from the lowlands of the North American east coast to as high as 15,000 feet (4,572m) in the Andes Mountains. In their constant search for food, they frequent a variety of habitats, including backyard feeders and gardens as well as deserts, mountain ranges, and forests. Their main requirement is a large supply of food—some visit more than 1,000 flowers per day in search of nectar. However, their feeding range varies dramatically. Some members of a species may confine themselves to a single blooming plant all day, hovering over its flowers, draining each one of nectar. Others may have fixed feeding routes that cover large distances, which they methodically fly in special patterns that define their territoriality and make them less vulnerable to predators. These predators include hawks, orioles, roadrunners, and other larger birds. Crows, jays, mice, and cats can also represent a danger to baby hummingbirds. There have even been cases of attacks on tiny hummingbirds by praying mantises, which remain perfectly still and camouflaged until the bird is just within their grasp.

Territoriality among hummingbirds can become a crucial, even violent issue, especially among South American species. These birds will stake out an area of nectar-rich flowering plants and defend its margins vehemently. Usually, dive-bombing accompanied by the loud shudder of wings is enough to defend the territory, but occasionally the hummer must resort to stabbing rivals with its beak.

Feeding often begins each day at the edge of a territory, where border defense is crucial. If the hummingbird removes all the nectar at these margins early in the day, it is less likely that other birds will make much headway infringing on the hummer's territory. Resources at a more interior location will meanwhile stay untouched, ready for a later feeding, and this smaller, inner area will be easier to defend.

Because hummingbirds have no sense of smell, they must find their food by sight. Nectar, sap,

Hummingbirds

RIGHT: *Here we see a sparkling violet-ear hummingbird feeding in an elongated hibiscus. The bird has moved so deeply into the flower to obtain nectar that its head is barely visible. Hummingbirds that feed in this way leave themselves vulnerable to any predators in the vicinity.*

and insects comprise their total diet. Young hummingbirds must learn to expect nectar from red-colored blossoms. Consequently, they are attracted to anything that is red and this can lead to disappointment. They tend, however, to learn quickly, establishing a close proprietorship to those blossoms that actually do yield nectar. They also learn to frequent areas where insects are abundant. Because a hummingbird can snatch its prey from the air, hummers have been seen flying through clouds of gnats or mosquitoes.

Hummingbirds are also attracted to water. They bathe in tiny rivulets, splatter wet leaves so that the droplets hit their bodies, or dart through clouds of mist.

Hummingbirds are not found in grassland plains, such as the Great Plains, which lack sufficient nectar-bearing plants to sustain their diet, and where vast open spaces would make them vulnerable to predators. They are also rare in marshes and shoreline habitats, and in mountain habitats higher than 9,000 feet (2,743m).

BELOW: Some hummingbirds claim a sizable territory, flying from flower to flower to feed, while others content themselves with a single plant. This rufous specimen appears to be guarding his food source between meals.

LEFT: A hummingbird and a sphinx moth dine together at a feeder. Both the sphinx moth and the hawk moth are sometimes mistaken for hummingbirds because of their similarities in size and feeding habits.

Physical Characteristics

Some hummingbirds rank as the smallest birds in the world, under three inches (7.6 cm) in length. The tiniest among their species is the bee hummingbird *(Mellisuga helenae)* of Cuba, about 2 1/4 inches (5.7cm) in length. Because of their small size and their ability to hover in the air, these birds have sometimes been mistaken for insects. The reverse is also true. Both the hawk moth and tree sphinx moth have been mistaken for hummingbirds, not only because of the coloring and size of these insects, but because their feeding habits and flight resemble those of these tiny hummingbirds.

Most hummingbirds appear to have areas of bright iridescent color, especially green. Another metallic color, such as red, blue, or another shade of green is apt to cover their throats. One exception is the hermit *(Phaethorninae)*, which is mostly brown. As with many birds, the males of the hummingbird species tend to be more brightly colored than the females.

LEFT: The Planalto hermit is one of about 40 hummingbird species that are not noted for their brilliant coloration. In fact, some of them are quite drab. Hermits are found in tropical forests.

OPPOSITE: One of the most fascinating characteristics of hummingbirds is their size. Their smallness is rarely captured adequately in photographs. Birds such as this ruby-throat average an astonishing 3 1/4 inches (8.25 cm), yet there are species which are even smaller.

Patterns and Colors

The jewel-like colors reflected from the bodies of hummingbirds are not produced by pigment variety. The top layers of feathers consist of tiny strands of tissue called barbules containing granules of melanin, which is a pigment, but which produces the many colors it itself does not possess by refracting the light. Light striking the barbules is refracted into iridescent colors much the same way that a prism divides white light into the many colors of the spectrum. Microscopic air bubbles hidden among the barbules also refract the light, creating iridescent effects. Two types of real pigments also exist in the feathers—reddish brown and black. Consequently, the color of a hummingbird's feathers changes dependent upon

RIGHT: The male broad-billed hummingbird is easy to spot. He has an iridescent blue throat that extends onto the upper breast, where it blends with the shimmering metallic green that covers the rest of the body.

OPPOSITE: Here we see not only the fineness of quality and richness of hue typical of hummingbird feathers, but also the characteristic iridescence. This effect is achieved both by the pigment within the feathers' structure and the refraction of light upon them.

RIGHT: *The rufous-tailed hummingbird is one of several tropical species that are occasionally spotted in the southern regions of the western United States. These rare visitors are not inhabitants of these areas, only tourists, and are known as 'accidentals.'*

the angle of incidence of the light striking it. Parts of its body can appear gleaming with rainbow colors and then suddenly turn black or dull brown when the angle of light no longer produces refraction.

How Flight Is Achieved

Hummingbirds have fewer feathers on their bodies than any other birds, in terms of sheer numbers, but the density of their feathers in relation to body size and weight is greater than that of many other birds. Adult hummingbirds lack down, the secondary set of feathers that is fluffier and lighter and that produces warmth. This lack conserves weight and contributes to their speed when flying, but also means that their metabolism must work extra hard to keep them warm.

Astonishingly strong chest muscles allow hummingbirds to reach wing-beat frequencies of up to 200 beats per second. These wing muscles take up as much as a third of the hummingbird's small body mass. The wings of a hummingbird can rotate only at the shoulder; the elbow and wrist

are fused. At the shoulder, the range of rotation is nearly 180 degrees. This allows the wings to stroke forward or backward, which they can do with nearly equal force, creating lift with no rotational or forward movement in a manner similar to a that of helicopter. In other birds, only the downward stroke can create lift or propel the bird forward. Their upstroke functions like a recovery stroke: they fall slightly and then are propelled forward again by the next downstroke. But the hummingbird reverses its wings as it accomplishes the upstroke, turning them upside down so that the upstroke also produces lift. This figure-eight pattern, in which the top edge always leads, allows the hummingbird to hover in the air, with no forward, backward, ascending, or descending movement. Using various methods of wing movement, a hummingbird can cruise up to speeds of thirty miles (38.2km) an hour or dive at speeds of up to about sixty miles (96.5km) an hour. It can change directions on a dime and even hover vertically in the air. Hummingbirds are also the only species of birds that can fly backward.

ABOVE: These amazing acrobats of the air not only feed, and sometimes mate, on the wing, but they can also fly upside down. These marvels are achieved through flight muscles that account for up to one-third of the bird's weight, enabling wing-beat frequencies of up to 200 beats per second.

Feeding and Vocalization

Hummingbird bills are custom designed to match the shape and length of the blossoms from which they draw nectar. They are the only bird species with an overlapping bill: the top half of the bill fits over the bottom half the way that a snug, overlapping cover fits a box. Bill shapes and lengths vary widely, but they usually tend to be long and narrow. Some are curved. Bills only open slightly, just enough to catch a flying insect, feed the young, or insert the long, bill-shaped tongue into the trumpet of a flower.

The long hummingbird tongue that fits so neatly inside the bill is designed for extracting nectar quickly and efficiently. Half of the tongue is divided into two tubes that end in fringes near the tip. When the tongue is extended, droplets of nectar adhere to the fringe and are drawn in by capillary action. Then the tongue is retracted, so that the nectar can be scraped off for ingestion, after which the tongue is extended into the flower again. This flicking action occurs about twelve times per second. Although the hummingbird can't smell nectar, it can taste it. About fifty taste buds alert it to the sugar concentration of any liquid it samples.

Once hummingbirds have swallowed their food, the food passes to an expandable sac in the neck known as a crop, which stores and supplies food in a way similar to that of the human stomach. The food passes gradually into the intestine, from which sugars can be drawn into the blood. Wastes produce a combination of urine and feces, which passes out of the body through an opening called the vent. To survive, a hummingbird must eat more than its weight in food each day. This makes their eating schedule a rather frantic one.

Anyone hoping that the hummingbird's song will be as aesthetically pleasing as this its plumage is likely to be disappointed. Most hummingbirds have limited vocalization, and some have none at all.

For this lack of vocal ability they substitute a variety of wing hums, which can be interspersed with wing pops, thumps, rattles, and even whistles.

Tropical hummers are more likely to sing with their throats than those in North America. The most musical is the drab hermit *(Phaethorninae)*, which even has the habit of participating in whole choruses with other members of its species. Anna's hummingbirds may be the second most musical, although the cacophonous song they use for courtship is not very pleasant to human ears. Lucifer *(Calothorozx lucifer)*, broad-billed *(Cyanthus latirostris)*, and blue-throated *(Lampornis clemenciae)* hummers all sing from time to time, seemingly in no regular or frequent pattern. A minority of birds produce sounds that humans would consider pleasant. The white-eared hummer *(Hylocharis leucotis)* can make a soft, bell-like sound. And the Allen's hummingbird *(Selasphorus sasin)* sometimes lets out a trill composed of multiple notes.

Black-chinned hummingbirds *(Archilocus alexandri)*—both mothers and babies—are extremely quiet during feeding. But after leaving the nest, the young are capable of making a high squeak, or other sharp call to attract their mother's attention when they are hungry or frightened. However, the majority of hummingbirds don't

ABOVE: Though hummingbirds are known to prefer red blossoms, they will also feed from yellow, orange, blue, and white flowers. This black-chinned hummer is enjoying a meal in Arizona's Sonora Desert.

OPPOSITE: Many plants depend on hummingbirds for the survival of their species. Having no way to disperse their pollen, the plants rely on the birds to transfer it on bills and feathers to other plants for pollination, thereby guaranteeing a new generation of plants.

FOLLOWING PAGE: A male magnificent hummingbird seems to be suspended in space as he hovers before a flower to feed.

ABOVE: Aside from color, hummingbirds choose flowers whose position and angle on the plant grants easy access for feeding. The sweetness of the plant's nectar is also a factor. Nectar that is too sweet is also too thick and not easy to extract.

used multiple high-pitched tones. They may just let out a single note, called a chip note, as they move from blossom to blossom to signal their presence to other hummingbirds. Most species are distinguished by the quality of that note. For example, Rufous hummingbirds make a sharp clicking sound, and broad-billed hummingbirds let out a rasp. When hummingbirds engage in aggressive behavior, which may be fairly frequent, their vocalizations are realized repeatedly and rapidly.

Because hummingbirds have very little down and very little body fat, they must rely on their hard-working metabolisms to keep them warm. Falling temperatures at night, when they are at rest, can represent a danger. This is especially the case since their frantic feeding schedule is suspended each night, and during those hours, the furnace of metabolism is not being stoked. A partial solution to this problem lies in the fact that hummingbirds are the only birds that become torpid. At night, if necessary, their body temperature can drop from its normal daytime temperature to as low as seventy degrees, often matching the temperature of the outside air. This ability allows them to conserve energy. Their heartbeat slows from normal levels—which during the day can reach 1,000 beats a minute—to levels as low as 159 beats a minute. Their breathing grinds to a near halt. If body temperature drops too low, the bird's metabolism may stoke up again, producing just enough heat to keep it from being harmed. At sunrise, they come out of their stupor. It takes about ten minutes for them fire up their metabolism, as their bodies go through a cycle of intense shivering and their heartbeat and breathing increases. At the end of this cycle, their temperatures have reached the minimum heat output associated with the energy for flight—about eighty-six degrees.

Food

Hummingbirds' need for constant food supplies has fine-tuned their migratory skills. When hummingbirds appear in an area, it means that the seasonal plants in that area are in bloom and are producing nectar. The only exception to this is during long flights of migration, when hummingbirds might suddenly find themselves out of synch with the blooming of local foliage. At such times, hummingbirds rely more heavily upon insects for nutrition, and are also more apt to experiment with unknown species of flowers.

RIGHT: This side view of a Lucifer hummingbird shows clearly the bird's long, slightly decurved beak. The beaks of various species have evol-ved to enable the birds to feed on the flowers most abundant in their particular habitat.

The flowers upon which hummingbirds feed have evolved along with them, so that each meets the specific needs of the other. To attract a hummingbird, a flower must be red or possibly yellow in color; it must bloom in the daytime, and it must be rich in nectar. It is also important that the flower lack any sort of "landing pad," a platform upon which competing birds could pearch while feeding. Flowers without such landing areas are accessible only by hummingbirds, which can hover and feed while hanging in the air. Another feature of blossoms frequented by hummingbirds is their shape. The nectar must be located at the base of a long tube protected by strong plant tissue, so that only the long, narrow bill of the hummingbird can then gain access to it, again eliminating competition from other birds. Trumpet or tubular shaped blossoms make perfect safeguards for hummingbird nectar. Scentless blossoms are also favored by hummingbirds, as scents may attract nectar-feeding animals with a sense of smell, once again increasing competition. In return for tailoring themselves to the needs of hummingbirds, these flowers receive a vital service. While the hummingbird feeds on nectar, pollen sticks to its beak, neck, and face to be transported to another blossom at the next feeding station. Without hummingbirds, these types of plants would be unable to reproduce.

In North America, hummingbirds are attracted to azalea bushes, mimosa, flowering quince, and large red buckeye trees, whose blossoms can feed dozens of birds in early spring. They love the trumpet-shaped flowers of the morning glory and have been seen hovering at cypress vines and Japanese honeysuckle. Hummingbirds love the nectar of the cardinal flower, as well as the lupine and the yucca. They feed from hanging fuschia blossoms, impatiens, red salvia, azaleas, and even petunias. They also frequent bee balm, delphinium, columbine, lupine, and butterfly bush plants. They've been seen feeding from lilacs, lilies, mint, sage, thistles, hollyhock, larkspur, and currant, as well as forty or so other North American flowers.

The insect menu of hummingbirds is equally eclectic, and depends upon their specific habitat. Hummingbirds are apt to eat flies, fruit flies, mosquitoes, aphids, ants, or spiders. If insects are available, a hummer may eat hundreds of them in one day. They may even raid a spider's web to make off with a captured insect or with the ruling predator himself. Tiny insects are sometimes in

BELOW: Open meadows and fields provide sustenance, not only to permanent and semi-permanent residents, but also to migratory hummers that stop off to feed and replenish their strength for the rest of the journey ahead.

ABOVE: *The Anna's hum-*

ABOVE: *The Anna's hum-mingbird is noted for singing from some conspicuous perch and then launching itself into a steep and spectacular display dive. Only males engage in this type of behavior.*

OPPOSITE: *This Brazilian hummingbird, a violet-capped woodnymph male, is seen in all his magnificence. Brilliant plumage is important for males in courtship displays. Females have less spectacular feathers, and are therefore able to blend into the forest when they are hatching their young and are extremely vulnerable.*

plentiful supply at the location of the nectar hummingbirds seek. They can pull them into their beaks the same way that they ingest nectar.

Because of their high metabolism, hummingbirds need between 6,000 and 12,000 calories per day. About seventy percent of this food comes in the form of liquefied sugar, and the rest from insect protein. A small amount of it can be stored as fat, but the energy needed for wing beats, licking, and body warmth quickly uses up a great deal of what they ingest. Hovering especially requires a great deal of energy. Their body extracts about ninety-seven percent of the sugars contained in nectar, which can be digested in less than an hour. Meanwhile, the water from the nectar is excreted in large amounts of urine. Thus, feeding, digesting, and excreting take up nearly the entire day. Even when the birds seem to be resting lazily on a branch, they are probably digesting food stored in their crops.

Courtship and Breeding

Hummingbirds are not lifetime maters. Adults are, in general, too competitive and too solitary to form permanent couples. They become interested in each other only when it is time to mate. To precipitate mating, the female becomes the aggressor. It is often she who begins looking for a male, once she has chosen a location for her nest and started to build it. Meanwhile, the males have established their own feeding territories, which they also intend to use to attract females. Males attract females by posing, flying in particular patterns, and creating vocal and wing sounds. Sometimes they dive toward females, or fly back and forth before them, showing off the iridescence of their feathers. They may also hover. Those that form singing choruses, or leks, most of which are confined to Latin America, work jointly to attract females. Hummingbirds may also entice a female by pantomiming the act of feeding. All in all, male

LEFT: *Hummingbirds are known for their fearlessness in confronting intruders that enter their territories. Aerial dogfights are common, and it is fascinating to watch the fierceness which these birds can summon in order to chase away other hummingbirds, bees, and birds larger than themselves.*

courting techniques are not that different from the gestures they undergo when defending their territory. They are attention-getting, and somewhat intimidating.

Actual intercourse is brief, though it may occur several times. It never occurs for more than a day between a particular couple. Once copulation is over, a female hummingbird has little use for a male. Now it is time for her to set about with the real business of gestation and parenting. In most cases, females build the nest, lay the eggs, and then incubate them on their own. They usually choose a location that is not in the feeding territory of males, opting for peace and quiet over optimum feeding locations, even if it means relying upon insects as the staple of their and their newborn's diet.

Aside from the hermit hummingbird, which builds long hanging nests, most hummingbirds build cup-like nests out of bark, moss, and leaves, which they fasten together with threads stolen from spider webs. Because these nests must be well concealed from predators, they require dense foliage, unless their location is so remote that visibility doesn't matter. Nests are made of two layers. On the outside are particles of twigs, grass, fur, bark, moss, and leaves, often held together by the filaments from the spider webs. The inner layer of the nest is a soft lining of fur, fluffy vegetation, or found bird feathers. If the nests are built near human habitations, they may include dryer lint, scraps of cloth, or human hair. Most importantly, they must be of a color and size that is easily camouflaged by their surroundings.

OPPOSITE: *Their are wide variations in the shape and length of hummingbird bills. The impressive sickle-like bill of this rufous-breasted hummingbird in French Guyana stands in marked contrast to the relatively short bill of the Costa's hummingbird.*

Hummingbirds

RIGHT: *Humming-birds' nests are excellently constructed, made of an array of nesting materials held together by a saliva glue. The hatchlings will be fed in the nest for three to four weeks before striking out on their own.*

RIGHT: *This female has chosen a spot in a tree that is shady and concealing, and therefore, relatively safe from predators. After mating, male hummingbirds take no part in raising the young. It is the female alone who builds the nest, hatches the eggs, and feeds the chicks.*

LEFT: *Young birds are well known for the noises they make, calling attention to themselves and demanding to be fed. Baby hummingbirds do not do this; they are completely silent. It has been suggested that this is a trait that has evolved to keep the chicks safe from any nearby predators that might be attracted by their calls.*

33

The eggs that hummingbirds lay are tiny, about the size of jelly beans, and their average incubation period, at least in North America, is about sixteen days. In almost every case, only two eggs are laid. Using techniques to warm the eggs with her body, to let them cool off, or to shade them from too much sun, the female manages to keep the eggs at a constant temperature of about ninety degrees, until they are ready to hatch.

Newborns are born blind and featherless, and are sheltered and kept warm with the bodies of their mother. Their mother must also gather nectar and insects to feed them until they can find food on their own. It takes a little more than three weeks for hummingbird babies to grow feathers and reach their adult size. Then they begin learning how to fly. Bills reach their full size a bit later. They then gradually they learn to feed themselves, instead of eating partially digested food from their mothers.

Most of the skills new adult hummingbirds need to survive they must learn on their own. They practice various flight maneuvers alone, and begin a trial-and-error search for food. Red blossoms seem to attract them by instinct, but only experimentation teaches them how to reach the nectar in each kind of flower. They learn how to avoid predators and how to keep their plumage in good condition by bathing and grooming it.

The raising of young and protection of hummingbird species is probably connected to a migratory phenomenon among these birds. Males migrate northward about three weeks earlier than the females. In the fall they leave before the females to travel south as well. It may be that the

RIGHT: *Blind and without feathers, this newly hatched chick lies beside the egg of its sibling. Since hummingbird eggs are laid a day or so apart, they do not hatch at the same time. For the first weeks of life, both will be totally dependent on their mother for food and warmth.*

males are protecting the females and their young from starvation by exploring the unknown terri tory on the migratory route in advance. Also, the females will find blossoms more fully mature when they arrive later. This will make the demands of feeding less intense for them and allow them time for nesting.

Hybrid mating is relatively rare among hummingbirds. It usually occurs only between closely related species who happen to be in the same habitat at the same time. Consequently, it is most likely to happen on the margins of breeding ranges, where a bird in search of a mate has sometimes strayed.

RIGHT: These two black-chinned chicks seem to be posing for a family portrait. They are well developed and will soon start making the first awkward attempts to fly and move about on their own. Once they have mastered their flight skills, they will leave the nest for good. This usually occurs about four weeks after hatching.

OPPOSITE: It takes about two weeks for hummingbird eggs to incubate and hatch. During that time the mother sits atop the eggs almost constantly, with only short breaks to feed, and thus maintain her energy and body heat. Incubation is aided by the soft insulating materials with which the nest is lined, holding in heat and keeping the eggs at a constant temperature.

ABOVE: *All seems to be going well as this mother feeds her thriving young. However, there are many possibilities for disaster. High winds, a severe storm, a sudden drop in temperature, or a predator's attack can take away young lives. When this happens, some hummingbirds breed again in the same season to replace the chicks they have lost.*

RIGHT: *Constant care and maintenance are necessary to keep dazzling plumage dazzling. Dust, parasites, fungi, and bacteria must be removed. A gland near the tail secretes a waxlike substance which is spread around the body with the bill, cleaning and polishing the feathers.*

LEFT: The largest hummingbird is appropriately called the giant hummingbird. Measuring about 8 1/2 inches (22cm)— about the size of a cardinal—it lives high in the Andes Mountains, and is, not surprisingly, the slowest flying hummingbird.

LEFT: Two rufous-tailed hatchlings sleep side by side in the nest while there mother is away gathering food. For the first few days, she will feed them mostly insects, providing the needed protein for growth. Gradually, as they become larger, she will introduce nectar into the diet.

FOLLOWING PAGE: Preferring a dry climate, as do other members of its species, this Costa's hummingbird has found a warm spot in a gnarled, dust-whitened tree on the Island of the Holy Spirit in the Sea of Cortez.

CHAPTER TWO

FAVORITES OF BIRDWATCHERS AND PHOTOGRAPHERS

Observing the Hummingbird

You might be surprised at how many opportunities there are for glimpsing hummingbirds, given their reputation as elusive and exotic treasures of nature. Bird lovers have been known to travel the world in search of these swift, shimmering creatures, searching the Grand Canyon, northern Florida, Mexico, and the Caribbean. Others have been astonished to find out, once they have learned to recognize hummingbirds, that these creatures have been frequenting their backyard gardens on a regular basis.

Nancy L. Newfield, a hummingbird enthusiast and specialist, offered several guidelines for observing these birds in a column she writes entitled "Hummer Notes." Newfield suggests that anyone looking for hummers pay special attention on nature walks to red-colored wildflowers; hummingbirds in the area are likely to have noticed them as well. Small creeks and streams are also good places to spot hummingbirds undergoing bathing rituals. And within clouds of insects hummingbirds may suddenly be revealed, darting around in search of dinner on the run.

Newfield also suggests that the hummingbird lover look for blossoms of salvia, calla lilies, bee balm, and other red flowers in those urban areas

ABOVE: A cardinal flower has attracted the hungry attention of a male broad-bill just outside Tucson, Arizona. Other flowers that attract hummingbirds in the Southwest are the scarlet monkeyflower, the scarlet bugler, and bouvardia.

OPPOSITE: There is a code that most nature photograph -ers instinctively observe. Their mission is to photograph wild creatures for others to view and to protect the integrity of the environment. Accordingly, the subjects must not be threatened or their activities interrupted, and their often fragile habitats must not be disturbed.

Hummingbirds

RIGHT: *Apart from several important locations in the American Southwest, where hummingbirds are easy to spot, the adventurous birder will find a visit to Costa Rica well worth the trip. The country has introduced an aggressive conservation program, preserving many vital habitats. This unique purple-throated mountain gem was photographed in the Costa Rican tropical cloud forest.*

RIGHT: *Most hummingbird enthusiasts and photographers have relatively easy access to the birds in North America. Observing more exotic species, however, requires dogged determination, such as that exhibited by the man who photographed this Brazilian ruby hummingbird feeding on an orchid in the heart of a rain forest.*

OPPOSITE: *For those who are horticulturally challenged and don't care to plant a garden to attract and observe hummingbirds, it is a good idea to learn about a few of the basic flowers that hummingbirds like, such as this trumpet creeper.*

that maintain nature centers, botanical gardens, or parks. Wearing a red article of clothing is also a good idea; a hummingbird may actually fly up to examine you, just to make sure you're not really a nectar-bearing flower. Above all, Newfield counsels the novice hummingbird observer to be patient. Hummers may not appear immediately, and lots of idle time may be necessary.

At what time of the year can one expect to see hummingbirds? In temperate climates hummingbirds arrive in the spring and leave in the fall, but as one moves from region to region of the United States, the parameters change. In the northeast, males, at least, begin the flight toward warmer climates in the first couple of weeks of September. In the St. Louis, Missouri area, the official date of departure is the middle of October. The Anna's hummingbird of the Pacific Coast and southern Arizona is likely to stick around well past the official start of the fall season. And the Allen's hummingbird can be seen year round on the Channel Islands and on the Palos Verdes Peninsula of southern California. In the Rocky Mountains, migration seems to follow a strict schedule. You can expect all hummingbirds to be gone by Labor Day. Likewise, ruby-throated hummingbirds will leave the north fairly promptly, but they may be content with going no further south than the Florida peninsula, where they will spend the winter. As mentioned before, other species, such as the rufous, the black-chinned, and the buff-bellied (*Amazilla yucatanensis*) may also go no further than the Gulf Coast for the winter.

If you really want to know where you can see hummingbirds in your area, consult a few migration charts. There are several available online that will give you an idea of when you can expect these visitors.

Attracting Hummingbirds

When it comes to attracting hummingbirds to your vicinity for close-up viewing pleasure, you can do a lot more than wear red clothing. In fact, your ability to provide allurements can even out-shine that of the hummer male during its breeding season. To lure the hummers in your neighborhood to your backyard, provide leafy bushes, trees, and nesting materials. These include ferns, moss, lichens, and leaves. Hummingbirds will be happiest if they can find both sunny and shaded areas. A gentle lawn sprinkler or patio fountain may also interest them.

Even if you decide to use a hummingbird feeder, as described below, you'll want to place it in an environment that is appealing to hummingbirds. Depending on how committed you are to providing a habitat for these creatures, you might consider creating an appealing and useful humming-bird environment by planting a hummingbird garden. Flowers that bloom at different times are ideal. A long blooming period will extend the time during which your garden is of value to the hummers. Your garden should also include plenty of twigs and stems, and a clothesline or badminton net for the birds to perch upon. Although these birds are expert hoverers, they spend as much as eighty percent of their time perching to digest food, rest, groom, or scan the vicinity for predators and rivals.

Think red when you think of sending out an invitation to hummers. Not only red flowers, but red garden furniture or statuary, even red surveyor's tape will attract them. Hummingbirds seem to respond strongly to ultraviolet light, and fluorescent surveyor's tape reflects a good deal of it. Setting out some ripe fruit can provide a special treat for your hummingbird visitors. They won't

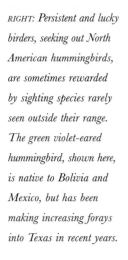

RIGHT: *Persistent and lucky birders, seeking out North American hummingbirds, are sometimes rewarded by sighting species rarely seen outside their range. The green violet-eared hummingbird, shown here, is native to Bolivia and Mexico, but has been making increasing forays into Texas in recent years.*

eat the fruit itself, but the fruit flies that eventually swarm around it will provide a welcome meal. Most importantly, don't use pesticides in your hummingbird garden—they can be lethal for these birds.

Of course, you should also emphasize red when it comes to a choice of trees, shrubs, vines, perennials, and annuals. Trumpet or tubular-shaped blossoms without odor and without "landing pads" that encourage other animals are a must. These plants depend upon hummingbirds for their pollination, and they have evolved to meet the skills and needs of hummingbirds at the exclusion of other animals. Ask your local nursery which plants are ornithophilous, a term for plants that depend upon birds to complete their life cycles.

The best way to ensure that the hummers in your vicinity will find your garden is to hang a hummingbird feeder. Maintaining and filling a hummingbird feeder correctly will do more for the species than attract them. It may also save

lives, supplementing the diet of a voracious hummer when other food sources are unavailable. You'll want to fill the feeder with a mixture of one part sugar to four parts water; use a little less sugar if your solution begins to attract bees. And don't use honey in your feeder—it may produce a fungus that can grow on the hummingbird's tongue, eventually killing it. It is also important that the solution is not colored with food dyes, which can harm the hummingbird's delicate system. It is also a good idea to boil your sugar-water solution for a few minutes, which will slow its fermentation.

At this time, there don't seem to be any totally reliable commercial feeding syrups on the market. Some that are available include a concoction of vitamins and minerals that is supposed to offer the hummingbird complete nutrition, but it's doubtful that this food alone can be substituted for the hummingbird's complex diet of nectar and various insects.

ABOVE: The average birder is fortunate to catch only a fleeting glimpse of an interesting species or to watch it from afar through binoculars. The great moments for the observer are the lucky finds, such as discovering a hummingbird taking a vigorous bath in a birdbath.

47

Choosing a Feeder

The feeders themselves are available in birding shops, garden centers, and by mail order. They may be made of plastic, glass, or ceramic. Make sure that you get one that is easy to clean. Perches, of course, are not necessary, but if you get a feeder with a perch, it may offer the driven, "Type A" hummingbird a needed respite from energy expenditure. The bird may take advantage of this and stay at the feeder for a longer time.

Choose a red feeder to attract the birds. Some people also recommend yellow, but hummers are less likely to respond to this color, which also hap-

pens to attract bees. Keep the feeder away from direct sunlight and strong winds, and replace the solution every few days, especially if the weather is hot. If the solution turns cloudy, replace it immediately. Clean the feeder regularly with hot water and a bottle brush, but don't use soap. About once a month, soak the feeder in a solution of 1/4 cup bleach to a gallon of water, for one hour. Then rinse well and let air dry.

Pests are likely to find your feeder, so you might want to take some precautions. Get a dripless feeder or one with a built-in ant trap on top. Or make your own ant trap by threading the wire

LEFT: Seven dazzling hummingbirds gather around a feeder in the Monteverde Cloud Forest Reserve in Costa Rica. Those that can be positively identified are two crowned brilliants (lower right), a purple-throated mountain gem (far left), and a copper-head emerald (left center).

used to hang your feeder through a spray-can top that you have punched near the edge with two holes and filled with vegetable oil. You may be able to avoid bees by painting over or removing any yellow-colored parts from your feeder. You can also purchase a feeder with bee guards. Or simply move a feeder or take it down for a day, and bees and wasps may forget about it. Hummingbirds won't.

Finally, be prepared for the possibility of sharing your feeder with bats. The disadvantage in this is that they eat so much that they can empty an entire feeder in one night. Use bee guards to discourage them, or take the feeder in at night. If you do this, however, you'll need to get it back out

to the hummers when they are hungriest, a little before sunrise.

If you're really a good friend to a hummer, you'll want to keep your feeder available for a week or two after the last hummer seems to have disappeared. In actuality, there may be some laggers still left behind. Subfreezing weather will quickly destroy any other possible sources of food.

If the temperature does dip suddenly, you may have to deal with freezing syrup in your feeder. Try warming it with a low-wattage flood lamp placed a few feet away from the feeder. If you live along certain areas of the California, Oregon, Washington, or Vancouver Island coast, you may

not want to disassemble your feeder at all. The Anna's hummingbird may stick around for the entire year, and the sugar you supply could be crucial for its survival.

How can you tell how many visitors you are really getting to your garden? According to Nancy L. Newfield, it may look like the same bird appearing and disappearing, and it may always perch in the same spot, but you may actually be seeing more than one bird. She recommends counting the number of birds in one location at a particular time and then multiplying by four. This is based upon the theory that the birds feed every fifteen minutes, so that those on feeding schedules during the other three fifteen-minute feeding periods of that hour will be absent from the location.

Photographing Hummingbirds

Photographing hummers brings rich rewards, but it is far from a simple procedure. The "flight-iness" of these birds coupled with the amazing speed of their wing beats makes them problematic portrait subjects. Nevertheless, photographers have managed to get some breathtaking pictures of hummingbirds in every situation: hovering, feeding, at rest, courting, and dealing with enemies and rivals.

If you decide to try to photograph hummingbirds, choose a camera that can focus up to about three feet. Forget about automatic focus—you'll probably find yourself in situations in which depth of field is too critical to rely on automatic. In fact, you'll need a setting with a fairly wide depth of field to compensate for the sudden

RIGHT: Calliope hummingbirds nest from mid-May to July, and during that time they may visit the backyard gardens of homes in Idaho, Montana, Wyoming, Washington, Oregon, California, and Nevada.

OPPOSITE: This delightful photo of a Costa's hummingbird, vigorously preening itself, was made by a photographer who traveled from Pennsylvania to Arizona specifically to observe and document hummingbird behavior. For the hummer enthusiast, Arizona offers several spots of interest, such as Cave Creek Canyon, Patagonia, Madera Canyon, and the Sonoran Desert Museum.

ABOVE: *Most hummingbird enthusiasts and photographers have relatively easy access to the birds in North America. Observing more exotic species, however, requires dogged determination, such as that exhibited by the man who photographed this Brazilian ruby hummingbird feeding on an orchid in the heart of a rain forest.*

ABOVE: The contribution of photography to the increased interest in birds and our ever-growing knowledge of them has been enormous within the past two decades. Not only their appearance but their behavior can now be documented. Here we see a swallow-tailed female feeding her young in Brazil.

positional shifts of the speedy hummingbird. This can be a problem. For closeups that provide life-size images, a very tiny aperture may be needed to get a depth of field that is even more than an inch. You'll also need a very fast shutter

RIGHT: The patient photographer who makes the trip to the Costa Rican rain forest will find an abundance of species and the opportunity to observe many different types of behavior, such as this male long-tailed hermit calling to females from his song perch at a lek site.

speed to prevent blurring. Choose very fast film and try to optimize your use of the available light by photographing on the right day and in the right areas of the garden, park, or natural habitat you've chosen. Be aware of the angle of incident light, and how it will affect the aperture setting of your camera.

You might want to use a flash, even in the daytime. To prevent ghosting, use a very powerful one. You might even be able to take some photographs at night if you can locate your hummers. Also, you might also have to practice capturing your hummingbird when it is at the right angle to the sun. Otherwise a bird that seemed like a sparkling jewel might turn out to look like a drab-feathered creature of a single hue.

LEFT: Hummingbirds move so quickly that it's hard to see and fully appreciate their acrobatic aerial maneuvers. Only through skilled photography can we capture their suppleness and the variety of contortions of which their bodies are capable.

OPPOSITE: Photographing hummingbirds in flight is challenging but ultimately rewarding, providing the added bonus to the individual of an intimate knowledge of these birds that can be gained in no other way. Making pictures of the birds at rest is also helpful for study and identification. Note the gradation of changing color in the back view of this blue-tailed sylph from the tropics.

CHAPTER THREE

AN A TO Z OF
HUMMINGBIRDS

North American Species

It would take a much thicker volume to fully illustrate the variety of all 341 hummingbird species. Their size ranges from the giant hummingbird *(Patagonia giagas)* of the Andes, which is about eight inches (20.3cm) long, to the minuscule Cuban bee hummingbird, which is a little over two inches (5cm). Hummingbird coloring can be as unexciting as that of the brown hermit hummingbird *(Phaethorninae)* or as eye-catching as the iridescent broad-billed, with its metallic-green-and-blue plumage. All members of the species have several features in common. These include ten tail feathers, ten primary wing feathers, and six secondary wing feathers. However, their bills differ in length, thickness, color, and degree of curvature.

This chapter profiles all of the fifteen hummingbirds native to North America. In addition to descriptions of each bird, information about their habitats and migrations is also provided, in hopes of giving readers in their vicinity an opportunity to observe them from time to time.

Allen's Hummingbird *(Selasphorus sasin)*

This straight-billed, dark-colored bird is one of the smallest hummers in North America, between 3 1/4 and 3 3/4

ABOVE: **Allen's hummingbird** *It's easy to see why this bird is often mistaken for the rufous hummingbird. Not only is the plumage coloring of the two species similar, but their vocal calls and wing-buzz sounds are so alike that they are almost identical.*

OPPOSITE: **Broad-billed hummingbird** *This bird grows to a length of 3 1/2 to 4 inches (9 to 10cm), and bears a resemblance to the white-eared hummingbird. Its low, dry call is similar to the ruby-crowned kinglet.*

ABOVE: **Anna's hum-
mingbird** *This full
front view clearly shows
the male Anna's charac-
teristic markings. These
birds grow to an average
size of 3 3/4 to 4 inches
(9.5 to 10cm).*

OPPOSITE: **Anna's hum-
mingbird** *West-coast city
dwellers sometimes have
the good fortune of spotting
this bird in their parks and
gardens. Not only is it a
year-round resident within
its range, but it is not shy of
the bustle of human activity.*

the Sierras. Some Allen's winter in the western half of Mexico and Baja California.

Allen's love open or wooded habitats and can be found feeding from blossoms in canyons, oak stands, chaparral, and willow and dogwood thickets. They are very territorial birds, and often in fierce competition with Anna's hummingbirds.

Anna's Hummingbird

(Calypte anna)

This large hummingbird has a green back and a red throat; it is the only North American hummingbird whose head is red. Its bill is straight, and its tail forks slightly when folded. Male Anna's are much more colorful than females. They have metallic violet or red on the throat and head, and green patches behind the eyes and back of the head. During mating they come forth with whole song patterns. Females have white-tipped wings and tail feathers and tend to have speckled throats.

The Anna's is a permanent resident of California, southern Nevada, Arizona, and other parts of the Southwest, with seasonal visits to the northwestern United States—Oregon, Washington, and western Nevada. There it hunts for insects or searches for tree sap. It also enjoys the nectar of fuchsias, red currant, Indian pinks, eucalyptus, and century plants, among others. These birds have been known to frequent urban areas.

Anna's were named in 1829 as a tribute to the beauty of Anna de Belle Massena, the Princess of Rivoli. The magnificent hummingbird, which is also known as Rivoli's hummingbird, was named after Anna de Belle Massena's husband, the Duke of Rivoli.

inches (8.25–9.5cm) in length. The males of this species are slightly smaller than the females. The sides of their chest and tail are reddish in color; in fact, until ornithologist Charles A. Allen (1841–1930) categorized them as a separate species, they had been confused with the rufous hummingbird *(S. rufus)*, despite the fact that a rufous does not have a metallic-green head and back. But immature male and female Allen's are almost indistinguishable from rufous.

Males of this species have red or orangeish chins and throat and metallic green-and-bronze heads; their wing feathers tend to be gray or dark brown. Females tend to have a spotted throat; their chests are white, mixed with brown, and their tail feathers are tipped with white.

Allen's hummingbirds frequent woody areas of Southern California and Los Angeles County, as well as the Channel Islands. From January through October, some may move north as far as southern Oregon or inland to

Black-chinned Hummingbird *(Archilochus alexandri)*

Black-chins are medium-sized hummers which are not particularly vocal. They have metallic-green backs, and somewhat resemble Costa's and Lucifer hummingbirds. The males have black throats mutating to metallic purple on their chins and throats. The heads of females are darker and duller than those of males, which have metallic-green heads.

The Black-chinned is a migratory bird, found from March through September in eastern Washington state, southern British Columbia, and Idaho, Oregon, California, Nevada, Utah, Colorado, Arizona, New Mexico, and Texas. They love meadows in mountain areas, forests, canyons, chaparral, and even some desert areas. They share territory with Costa's hummingbirds and, in Texas, with the ruby-throated hummingbird.

ABOVE: **Black-chinned hummingbird** *Aside from their characteristic black chins, these birds can be identified by their notched tails and bills that are slightly decurved. Their average body length is 3 to 3 1/2 inches (7.5 to 9cm).*

OPPOSITE: **Black-chinned humming-bird** *Males of this species are noted for what is called a 'dry buzz' sound which their wings make in flight. They can also be observed in flight displays that trace a gently arcing flight pattern.*

61

RIGHT: **Blue-throated hummingbird** *One distinguishing characteristic of both male and female blue-throats is a long wide tail with sizable white patches at the tips of the tail feathers. This can be helpful to birders, since females lack the distinctive blue-throat patch possessed by males.*

RIGHT: **Blue-throated hummingbird** *With its iridescent blue gorgetor neck marking, its relatively large size, and long beak, this is perhaps the easiest of all the hummingbirds to identify. Another species, the magnificent hummingbird, lives within its range, and there is often conflict between the two.*

Blue-throated Hummingbird
(Lampornis clemenciae)

As hummingbirds go, these are some of the largest in North America—reaching lengths up to 5 1/4 inches (13.3cm). They have long, straight bills. Males have a metallic-blue chin and throat; their heads, backs, chest, and abdomens are a dull metallic green, and their tails are dark green with white edges on the tips. Females resemble males, but lack the blue throat patch.

These birds feed heavily on insects. They are also attracted by the blossoms of tree tobacco, lobelia, agave, sage, and the cardinal flower. Their calls, which they utter in flight or while feeding or resting, are loud and high-pitched. They can be found in woodlands near streams or desert mountains in southwestern Arizona, New Mexico, and Texas. They winter in central Mexico.

These birds are very aggressive. They engage in standoffs with other species, such as the magnificent, the violet-crowned, and the black-chinned.

Broad-billed Hummingbird

(Cyanthus latirostris)

Broad-billed hummingbirds can be easily recognized. These birds by their loud, raspy cry, which sounds like two syllables: "yet-it! yet-it!" They also have a red bill which is wider than that of other hummingbirds. Their long tail ends in spiky shapes.

Broad-bills nest close to the ground in very small nests made of leaves, stems, and flower blossoms. Males have metallic-blue chins and throats, heads ranging from green to bronze-green, and

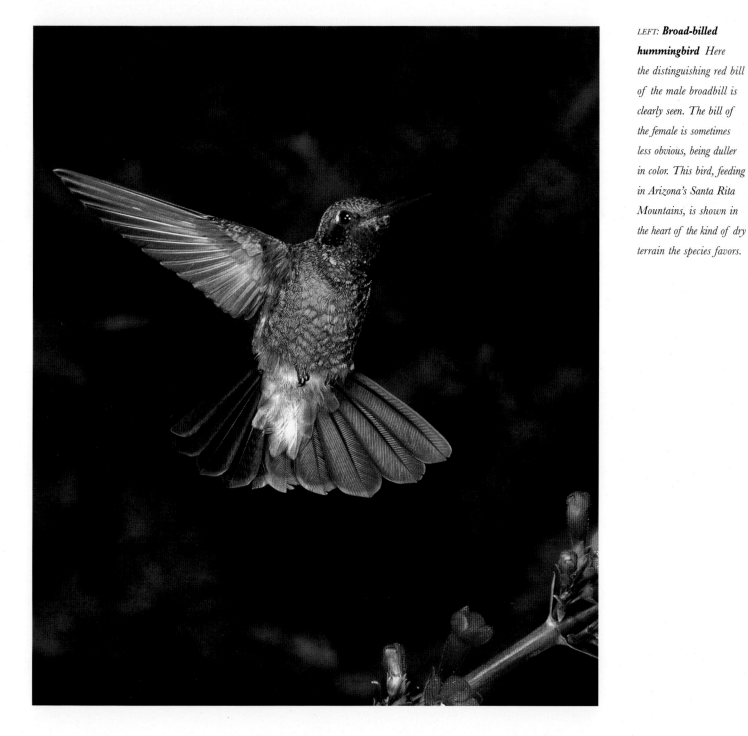

LEFT: **Broad-billed hummingbird** *Here the distinguishing red bill of the male broadbill is clearly seen. The bill of the female is sometimes less obvious, being duller in color. This bird, feeding in Arizona's Santa Rita Mountains, is shown in the heart of the kind of dry terrain the species favors.*

dark tails with white or grayish undertails. Females have dull metallic-green heads, backs, sides, and abdomens, and may be more gray-brown in color than males.

Wintering in southern Mexico, broad-billed hummers spend March through September in southern Arizona, southwestern New Mexico, and southwestern Texas. A few have been seen in southern California and Louisiana as well. They love canyons located near water. During courtship the male produces a distinctive buzzing sound with its wings.

Broad-tailed Hummingbird

(Selasphorus platycercus)

These medium-sized hummingbirds are extremely territorial. It is sometimes possible to spy the males surveying their domain from high tree perches. Their wings make a louder hum than those of most other hummingbirds.

Broad-tails prefer aspen, pinon, and juniper woodland near water. Wintering in southern and central Mexico, in March they fly north to Idaho, eastern California, and parts of Oregon, Nevada, Utah, Wyoming, Colorado, Arizona, New Mexico, and Texas.

Their chirping call is rather musical for a hummingbird. The males have bright, metallic-red chins and throats, and green or bronze-green metallic heads and backs. Females have whitish chins and throats, and their abdomens are a dull gray fading to buff. Both sexes are about the same in size.

Buff-bellied Hummingbird

(Amazila yucatanensis)

Also called the fawn-breasted hummingbird, these 4– to 4 1/2–inch (10.2 to 11.4cm) birds inhabit scrub areas and open woodlands as well as gardens and orchards in southern Texas, the Gulf Coast of Texas and Mexico, and the Yucatan peninsula in the spring and fall. They winter in the Gulf regions of Mexico and the Yucatan. In fact, their scientific species name, *Yucatanensis*, literally means "from the Yucatan."

The wings of these birds have a louder hum than most other North American hummingbirds. They are rather large, with metallic-green backs and heads, with long, red, slightly downward curved bills. The female is slightly smaller than the male, but both sexes share very similar coloring.

The first buff-bellied was discovered and named by an American ornithologist named Harry Oberholser, who observed a captured specimen near Brownsville, Texas in 1898. Because of its tail color, some people confuse this hummer with the rufous, even though the rufous has a red throat.

ABOVE: **Broad-tailed hummingbird** *A migratory bird, the broad-tail has an extensive range that stretches from Idaho and Wyoming, southward into Mexico and Guatemala. It prefers mountainous regions and is capable of surviving the cold nighttime temperatures of these places.*

LEFT: **Buff-bellied hummingbird** *Preferring to nest in small trees and dense undergrowth, this bird's range for the most part covers the Gulf coastal areas of Mexico, Guatemala, and Belize. It is seen in small numbers in the United States only in southern Texas and coastal Louisiana.*

Calliope Hummingbird (*Stellula calliope*)
Calliopes are North America's smallest hummer. They have metallic-green backs and heads and a short tail with square tips. The chin and throat of the male is dark, metallic purplish-red, sometimes combined with white to produce a vertical striped effect. Females have white chins and throats.

During courtship, the males makes U-shaped dives, ending the dive with a distinctive vocalization. They are very territorial, and aren't afraid to face off with larger birds. They are expert insect trappers, able to seize them in their bills while in flight.

Calliopes survive in meadows or in conifer and hardwood forests up to an altitude of 10,000 feet (3,048m), often building their nests among the pine cones. Migratory birds appear from March to September in British Columbia and western Alberta as well as Washington, Idaho, western Montana, western Wyoming, Oregon, and parts of California, Nevada, and Utah.

The birds are named for Calliope, one of the nine muses of ancient Greek mythology. Calliope's intellectual domain was poetry and eloquence.

RIGHT: **Calliope hummingbird** *Here are clearly seen the distinctive magenta stripes that color the throat of the male Calliope. As with most species, the female does not have such brilliant markings, and in fact, is less colorful overall than the male.*

OPPOSITE: **Calliope hummingbird** *Measuring 2 3/4 to 3 inches (7 to 7.5cm), the Calliope is the smallest hummingbird in North America. Its diminutive size, however, does not keep it from migrating great distances, traveling from its winter home in Mexico to the mountains of western Canada to breed each spring.*

Costa's Hummingbird *(Calypte costae)*
Also called the coast hummingbird or the ruffed
hummingbird, there are Costa's living year long
in southeastern California. Other migratory
Costa's come to southern California, southern
Nevada, western Arizona, Baja California, and
northwestern New Mexico from January through
October. A few have been seen in other western
states, such as Texas, New Mexico, and Oregon.
These birds love desert areas away from water
sources, where they survive on such desert plants
as mesquite, desert lavender, and desert willow.

The males of this species have a distinctive
metallic-purple chin, throat, and head; long feathers run from their throat down along their chest.
The females have white chins and throats and dull
metallic-green backs and heads. These birds have
developed a distinctive hovering style in which
they pump their tails up and down.

This bird was named in honor of Louis Marie
Pantaleon Costa (1806–1864), also known as the
Marquis de Beauregard. Costa had a large collec-
tion of hummingbird specimens. In 1839 Jule
Borcier, a naturalist, found the first specimen in
Baja California and named it after Costa.

Lucifer Hummingbird *(Calothorax lucifer)*
No devilish intention led to the naming of this
bird. The name is rather a tribute to the iridescent
beauty of hummingbirds, for "lucifer" also means
"bringer of light." Lucifers have long, dark,
downward-curving bills. They are small, and their
long tail produces a fork when it is folded. The
males have metallic-purple chins and throats, a
color that extends in long feathers along the sides

of the head down toward the chest. Females have white or grayish chins and throats, and a patch of black shading the area behind the eye.

Their call is quiet and high-pitched. Males court by flying back and forth before the female, while she waits in her nest. Surviving on plants and insects on desert plateaus and mountain slopes, they live in southwestern Texas, southeastern Arizona, and southern New Mexico from March to November, spending their winters in central Mexico.

Magnificent Hummingbird *(Eugenes fulgens)*
These large hummingbirds, which were once known as Rivoli's hummingbirds, have long, fairly straight, dark bills. Their metallic-green plumage is somewhat darker than that of other hummingbirds. The males have metallic-green chins and throats and purple heads. The females have whitish chins and throats and dull green heads and backs.

The chirping call of these birds is loud and musical. They live in oak or conifer forests near streams and mountain slopes where they are only mildly territorial, spending quite a bit of time perched high above their feeding territory. In April they migrate from central Mexico and Central America to western New Mexico and southeastern Arizona, where they stay through November.

FOLLOWING PAGE:
Magnificent humming-bird *This species, though relatively large in size, is considered much less aggressive than other hummingbirds. The male's deep purple cap on the head and brilliant green throat make it fairly easy to identify in the field.*

LEFT: ***Lucifer humming-bird*** *This hummingbird is by no means abundant in the United States. It favors dry areas, and therefore is found in pockets in such places as the most southerly portions of Texas, New Mexico, and Arizona, where it is associated with the agave, or century plant.*

OPPOSITE: ***Magnificent hummingbird*** *As hummingbirds go, the magnificent is considered large, measuring around 4 1/2 to 5 inches (11.5 to 12.5cm) in length. Overall, its coloring is dark in comparison to its more brilliant and resplendent cousins. This feature has caused it to be described among hummingbird fanciers as 'The Black Knight.'*

Ruby-throated Hummingbird *(Archilochus colubris)*

These are the only hummers found regularly east of the Mississippi. Both the males and the females of this species are markedly territorial, the males engaging in display fights in a wave pattern. Their call sounds like a high-pitched squeak, and their bills are dark and long.

The males have a ruby-red metallic chin and throat, and a whitish chest with green shading along the sides. The females have a white chin and throat, and a whitish gray or buff chest and abdomen.

These birds increase their normal body weight before they migrate to central and southern Mexico, Central America, or the Gulf states for the winter. They spend March through October in the East, from Canada to the Gulf of Mexico and inland as far as the Mississippi. Here they frequent hardwood and conifer forests and wetlands, as well as parks and gardens in suburban and urban areas. They mate from spring to early summer, building their nests of plant detritus and mud, which they attach to branches with spider filament.

ABOVE: **Ruby-throated hummingbird**

Measuring a mere 3 1/4 to 3 1/2 inches (8 to 9cm), the ruby-throat is nonetheless a determined and aggressive defender of its territory, producing a loud wing sound as it swoops through its threat displays to drive off intruders. In addition to flowers and insects, this bird is also known to feed on tree sap, as do a number of other species.

OPPOSITE: **Ruby-throated hummingbird**

The fact that it thrives in public parks and private gardens, as well as in wild areas, has made the ruby-throat a favorite among birdwatchers, particularly in the eastern United States. Since it is the only hummer consistently found in abundance in that region, it is particularly cherished.

*ABOVE: **Rufous hummingbird** A detail of the iridescent gorget of the male rufous hummingbird. Females of the species lack this mark, and have instead small reddish and greenish spots on the throat. The length of these birds is 3 1/4 to 3 1/2 inches (8 to 9cm).*

*RIGHT: **Rufous hummingbird** This beautifully colored reddish bird migrates annually in the spring from Mexico to western North American areas, reaching as far north as southern Alaska. The distinctive buzzing of its wings is well known to gardeners and nature lovers in these areas. Here the characteristic markings of the male are shown.*

Rufous Hummingbird *(Selasphorus rufus)*

This is the only North American hummingbird with a rufous (reddish) color on its head and back. The male of the species is slightly smaller than the female. The male has a metallic-red chin and throat, and its head is a dull metallic bronze-green or bronze. The female's chin and

throat are spotted. Its head and back are a dull metallic bronze-green.

These birds inhabit forests, chaparral, and meadows inland and on the coast above the timberline. They are recognizable by the rattling and buzzing sounds their wings make when they are courting. They build their nests from plant fiber and disguise them with bark and lichen so that they look like part of a tree.

From February through October, the rufous are found from southern Alaska through western Canada, Washington, Oregon, Idaho, and Montana in the north, and as far south as southern Mexico. They winter in Mexico and in the southwestern United States. During migration, they have been known to fly from the Alaskan coast to central Mexico in a wide elliptical path, which may be the longest migration undergone by any bird—thirty to forty degrees in latitude.

Violet-crowned Hummingbird

(Amazilia violiceps)

Also known as the azure-crowned hummingbird, this large hummer can be identified partly by its long, slightly downward-curved bill, which is red with a dark tip. The males have a purple head and a white chin, throat, chest, and abdomen. Females look like a drabber version of the same pattern. Their chattering call is sharp and metallic.

From June through September, violet crowns reside in a small area between the border of southwestern New Mexico and southeastern Arizona. A few have been spotted in Arizona, California, and Texas.

Violet-crowned hummers love cottonwood and sycamore groves. They frequent canyons and arroyos, where they feed on agave—the century plant—and other plants of the dry southwest. Little is known about their courtship habits.

LEFT: **Violet-crowned hummingbird**
Measuring 4 inches (10cm) in length, this striking bird, unfortunately, is found in the United States only in small areas of southern Arizona and New Mexico. These are breeding sites for a limited number of individuals that migrate north from Mexico. Here a male of the species is seen.

ABOVE: **White-eared hummingbird** *Large numbers of these birds occur in the mountainous regions of northern Mexico. However, they are scarce in the United States. The best chances for finding them are in the most southerly areas of southeastern Arizona, though they can occasionally be seen in southern New Mexico and southern Texas.*

OPPOSITE: **White-eared hummingbird** *With its identifying white head-streak and red bill, this white-ear is browsing among the blossoms in Arizona's Madera Canyon. Places such as this are the preferred feeding and breeding grounds of this mountain species, which measures an average 3 1/2 inches (9cm) in length.*

White-eared hummingbird (*Hylocharis leucotis*)

The most unusual feature of this bird is the white stripe that begins behind its eye and curves down the side of its head. Its bill is reddish, tipped in black. Males have metallic-blue or violet heads and metallic-green throats. The females have spotted chests and throats. Males are slightly larger than females. Both sexes fan their tails while hovering and feeding.

White-ears survive in scrub habitat in oak and pine forests, where they feed on small winged insects and many types of flowers. The males congregate in groups called leks; they share mating territory and attract females by singing as a group. Their song is pleasant and bell-like. Once the mating ritual begins, males and females pair up for winged acrobatics.

Most North American white-ears appear in the extreme southeastern part of Arizona. During the winter they live in the mountains of Central America and central Mexico in the Sierras.

INDEX